One Sheet, Big Results:
Winning Strategies Unveiled, Your Recipe for Success.

Stephen S. Anderson

Table of contents.

Introduction

It's an ordinary morning, and you're tasting your espresso while looking at your messages. You open one, and it's a language loaded message from an organization attempting to sell you their best in class item. Chances are, you'll raise a ruckus around the town button before you even completion that first taste. Presently, envision getting a basic, clear, and succinct message that comes to the heart of the matter. Abruptly, you're charmed and need to find out more. This is the force of straightforwardness.\

In this present reality where we're besieged by data and intricacy, straightforwardness stands apart as a signal of clearness. It resembles a much needed refresher in a brown haze filled city, or a cool glass of water on a singing summer day. In business and promoting, straightforwardness can be the way to opening unrivaled achievement and making enduring associations with clients.

In this article, we'll leave on an excursion to investigate the significance of straightforwardness at each level of the business and promoting chain. En route, we'll share genuine models from less popular organizations that have saddled the force of straightforwardness to accomplish unimaginable outcomes. We'll likewise give reasonable direction to assist you with meshing this extraordinary guideline into the texture of your own association. In this way, lock in, and we should plunge into the entrancing universe of effortlessness.

The Advantages of Executing Straightforwardness Across the Association
1. Imagine yourself at a jam-packed evening gathering. The room is loaded up with giggling, ringing glasses, and enlivened discussion. However, in the midst of the racket, you end up attracted to a tranquil, smart visitor in the corner. Their words, however few, are spellbinding and savvy, making you anxious to hear more. In the clamor of current business, straightforwardness resembles that visitor — a voice of clearness and shrewdness that slices through the commotion.

2. Carrying out straightforwardness across an association can yield wonderful advantages, from cultivating better correspondence to expanding proficiency and pleasing clients. We should investigate the manners by which effortlessness can lift a business higher than ever.

3. Further developed correspondence and cooperation
Effortlessness energizes open, genuine, and direct correspondence, behaving like an extension between colleagues with different foundations and skill. At the point when everybody communicates in similar language, grasping twists, and cooperation blooms. Consider a little tech startup, InnovateX, which took on a "no-language" strategy in group gatherings. The outcome? A more comprehensive and cooperative climate that started splendid thoughts and cultivated a genuine feeling of brotherhood.

4. Expanded productivity and decreased intricacy
Like an expert gourmet specialist who skillfully uses a blade to make culinary show-stoppers, effortlessness permits organizations to slice

through intricacy and smooth out processes. By cutting back the excess and zeroing in on the main thing, associations can open secret efficiencies and enable representatives to take care of their best responsibilities. Take the instance of a nearby publicizing organization, AdCrafters, that embraced a "toning it down would be ideal" reasoning in their task the board approach. The result was a less fatty, more coordinated group that reliably conveyed uncommon work on time and on financial plan.

5. Improved client experience and fulfillment
In our current reality where decision proliferates, straightforwardness is a gift that clients treasure. By offering clear, straightforward items and administrations, organizations can make positive, essential encounters that make clients want more and more. For instance, a non mainstream book shop, PageTurners, worked on their in-store design and item classes, making it a breeze for clients to see as their next extraordinary read. The outcome? A reliable client base and rave surveys via online entertainment.

6. More engaged independent direction and technique execution
At the point when you strip away the superfluous, what remains is the substance of the main thing. Straightforwardness empowers organizations to focus on their center goals, considering more exact navigation and compelling system execution. A little design brand, ChicThreads, fills in as a brilliant illustration. By working on their item contributions and advertising methodology, they had the option to zero in on their remarkable selling focuses and quickly develop their client base.

By embracing straightforwardness, associations can saddle its extraordinary power and shown themselves a way to getting through progress. As the maxim goes, "Straightforwardness is a definitive complexity," and there could be no greater time than now to make it a fundamental piece of your business.

Applying Straightforwardness to Various Degrees of Business and Promoting

Envision an expert painter, cautiously choosing each shade and brushstroke to make a stunning show-stopper. Like the craftsman, a business can apply the standard of straightforwardness to different parts of its tasks, creating a strong and harmonie.

Chapter1:

Target audience.

What Is a Target Audience?

A target audience is a group of people defined by certain demographics and behavior. Your main interest group alludes to the particular gathering of buyers probably going to need your item or administration, and in this manner, the gathering who ought to see your promotion crusades. Interest groups might be directed by age, orientation, pay, area, interests or a horde of different elements. A decent showcasing plan should have the option to "construct" your main interest group — recognizing your client's socioeconomics and sorting out which instruments will best draw in them — "they" will come.

Then, at that point, center around the best client for your business. Numerous entrepreneurs tragically imagine that their item or administration is appropriate for everybody. For instance, focusing on Facebook Advertisements to "all" (sexes, ages, and so on) when your item is obviously for ladies more than forty doesn't appear to be legit. Not exclusively is publicizing to everybody seldom legitimate, however it can really hurt your promoting endeavors by irritating individuals and squandering your publicizing spending plan superfluously..

steps to identify your target audience:

1.An interest group alludes to) Decide your client's socioeconomics. Except if you're selling oxygen, not every person needs your item or administration. So who does? Men or ladies? Old or youthful? Moderate or liberal? What is their financial section, instruction level, and interests? Whenever you've limited the rules down, it's much simpler to zero in your promoting system on the people who are probably going to require what you are advertising.

2) Decide your client's necessities. Since you have an unmistakable thought regarding the kind of individual you'll target, you'll need to

recognize their particular requirements with regards to what your business is advertising. All in all, what is the issue they are having that your item or administration is the answer for? By imagining their perspective and posing the inquiries they will have, you'll have the option to address their interests in your response — your showcasing message — before they happen.

3) Decide how your client will find out about you. We as a whole have companions who favor messaging to calling, so we realize that not every person is open to similar methods of correspondence. Is your ideal client more seasoned? Then you might need to run print promotions. On the off chance that they're Recent college grads who have never at any point pursued a paper, you might need to run Twitter promotions. Is your crowd nearby or worldwide? Could it be said that they are a stylish pack or a specialty swarm? The most ideal way to arrive at your interest group is through the channels from which they get their data as of now.

4) Expect your clients to be portable. Nowadays an ever increasing number of individuals are interfacing with the world through their cell phones, whether it's to understand news, shop or convey. As a matter of fact, tech expert Mary Meeker found that cell phones are surpassing any remaining gadgets, particularly the work area or PC, Web use. Of the 2.8 billion Web clients around the world, 2.1 billion are portable, a 23 percent increment from the year before. So anyway you arrive at your interest group, ensure you incorporate versatile promoting.

5. Lead Statistical surveying and Distinguish Industry Patterns
Take a gander at the statistical surveying for your industry to figure out where there are openings in help that your item can fill. Take a gander at patterns so that comparable items might see where they are centering endeavors, then sharpen in addition on your items' novel worth.

6. Dissect Contenders
Advertisers can glean some significant experience by taking a gander at contenders to see what their identity is regularly offering to, and how they go about it. Is it true or not that they are utilizing the web or disconnected

channels? Is it true or not that they are zeroing in on the chief or the ally?How to Identify and Market to your Target Audience.

1) Publish content to all social media. Social media is the new marketplace, so it's in your best interest to market your message via the social platforms on which your target audience is already spending time. In other words, don't waste time reaching out on Twitter if your target demographics are primarily on LinkedIn. Business Insider and LinkedIn break down the demographics of the major social networks:

- **Facebook**: 1.32 billion users, both male and female, between the ages of 18-54, and interested in consumer goods more than luxury goods.
- Twitter: 271 million users, primarily male, between the ages of 18-29, and are interested in getting their news via this network.
- **LinkedIn**: 300 million users, both male and female, between the ages of 30-64, and are highly-educated professionals with good incomes.
- **Pinterest**: 70 million users, primarily female, between the ages of 18-49, and interested in food, drink, and family/parenting content. Effective platform for visual-based products and services.
- **Instagram**: 200 million users, primarily female, between 18-29, and interested in clothing, accessories, and entertainment-related themes. Like Pinterest, it is very good for visual marketing.

2) Purchase online ads. If you have the budget, online advertising should be part of your marketing strategy, but choose a platform on which your target customers spend their time. According to Rocco Baldassarre, CEO of Zebra Advertisement:

The Bing Network or Google is ideal for traditional service providers because their audience is already looking for them and tend to convert easily. Using highly-targeted keywords works very well with search engine ads.

Display ads, such as Google AdWords, are best for a market who doesn't necessarily know about you. When they go to similar websites, your targeted ads will appear for them, and even if they don't click on your ad, it still raises brand awareness.

Facebook and Twitter ads are great if you are selling lifestyle products as they work by targeting customers by their behavioral patterns and interests. Like Google ads, even if your audience doesn't click on the link, they're still being exposed to your business.
LinkedIn advertising is perfect for B2B (business-to-business) services or products as it is able to target specific professions.

3) Make use of your brand advocates. According to a Nielsen study, 92 percent of people say they trust the recommendations they receive from friends and family more than any other form of advertising. Because of this fact, it behooves you to make use of this social proof and "partner" with your most loyal customers to get the word out. Brand advocates are those people, often repeat customers, who have purchased your product or service, love it, and enjoy talking about it. Be sure to get a testimonial from them and post it on your website; these personal statements tend to naturally describe the benefits and features of your product in a way that doesn't come across as selling. Offer your brand advocates small freebies, a discount on their next purchase, or a coupon for every referral they drive your way.

4) Co-market with similar brands. Do some research to find companies that share your audience without overstepping their business boundaries. For example, if you sell baby blankets, co-marketing with pre- and post-natal fitness centers can benefit both companies without taking business away from either of you. You can guest post on each other's blogs, share each other's social media posts, co-host contests and giveaways, and offer special discount coupons for each other's customers.

5) Encourage social networking in the office. A big part of the new online landscape is based on sharing. Diamond Strategic Marketing suggests having the whole team be involved in outreach, not just the marketing people, as it can lead to genuine, personal "marketing" of your business's

product or service (assuming your employees like and use what you're selling).

Chapter 2:

Crafting your value proposition

Your incentive structures the center of your plan of action. Without an incentive, it is difficult to be aware if and how your business will bring in cash, which accomplices you want, the idea of your key tasks, and how you will gain and hold clients. The motivation behind this exercise manual is to help you through the most common way of making an incentive for your business. Download and utilize this exercise manual to: In the present cutthroat business scene, standing apart from the group is fundamental for progress. Just 85% of organizations have laid out incentives. In this blog entry, we'll jump into what an offer is, the reason it is significant for your business, how you can distinguish one for your own image, and whether a current organization can find another offer. In the event that you don't have an unmistakable message, you will essentially pursue clients away!

What is an offer?

At its center, an incentive is a brief explanation that conveys the exceptional advantages and worth your item or administration offers to clients. It characterizes the motivation behind why clients ought to pick your image over rivals. A solid incentive tends to the trouble spots of your interest group, exhibits how your contribution takes care of their concerns, and features the worth they will acquire from picking your image.

 your image's validity and constructs entrust with your crowd.Making incentives isn't only for new organizations, it's likewise basic for laid out organizations to rethink their offers to remain significant The most effective method to find an incentive for your business:

Creating an incentive takes a little work. However, her are a few stages you can take to get clear on your informing:

Distinguish Client Needs: Comprehend the trouble spots, wants, and yearnings of your interest group. Direct statistical surveying, accumulate client input, and investigate industry patterns to acquire experiences into what makes the biggest difference to your clients.

2. Evaluate Contenders: Study your rivals' offers to recognize holes and open doors. Decide how you can separate your contribution and offer exceptional benefits that others in the market are not conveying.

3. Characterize Remarkable Selling Focuses: Distinguish the key elements, advantages, or arrangements your image offers that are particular from contenders. Feature what makes your item or administration unique and how it tackles client issues all the more actually.

4. Make a Convincing Assertion: Join your special offering with enticing language to make a brief and significant incentive assertion. Guarantee that it obviously imparts the advantages clients will insight and resounds with their necessities and goals.

Creating a strong offer is a continuous cycle that requires persistent refinement and variation to guarantee it stays pertinent and significant in a consistently developing business scene.

Making incentives isn't only for new organizations, it's likewise basic for laid out organizations to rethink their offers to remain applicable and cutthroat as business sectors shift and change. Developing client inclinations, mechanical progressions, and industry patterns offer endless open doors for improving marks of separation.

By proactively assembling and examining information, for example, client input, directing normal statistical surveying, and remaining very much educated regarding industry improvements, organizations can reveal new points of view on incentives that are lined up with changing client needs and developing business sector requests.

Making a strong offer is a continuous cycle that requires constant refinement and variation to guarantee it stays important and effective in a consistently developing business scene. By putting time and exertion into creating and conveying a remarkable offer, you position your image for progress and make a convincing justification behind clients to pick you.

A very much created incentive fills in as the foundation of effective marking. It separates your image, draws in your interest group, and lays out an upper hand. By understanding the significance of an incentive, distinguishing client needs, evaluating contenders, and creating a convincing assertion, organizations can situate themselves for development and client devotion.

Keep in mind, even settled organizations can find new offers by remaining sensitive to developing business sector elements. Thus, open the force of an extraordinary incentive and push your image higher than ever level of progress.

CHAPTER 3:

Reaching more customers

In order to boost revenue and develop a stronger market presence, businesses constantly work to broaden their consumer base. In this chapter, we'll examine a number of tactics that companies can use to successfully reach and interact with a broader audience.

- . Embrace digital marketing: In the age of the internet, having a presence online is essential. To reach potential customers, make use of social media platforms, SEO, content marketing, and email marketing. A larger audience might be drawn in via interesting content and clever ad placements.

Utilize influencer marketing by partnering with influencers who have a sizable fan base in your sector. Their support may help spread awareness of your company to a more substantial and receptive audience, enhancing credibility.

- **Increase Product Offerings**:

Diversify your line of goods and services to appeal to a wider group of clients. Your attraction is increased and your clientele is increased when you cater to different demands and tastes.

- **Improve Customer Experience:**

Happy customers are more inclined to recommend businesses when they receive excellent customer service and individualized treatment. Word-of-mouth advertising continues to be effective.

- Turn devoted customers into brand promoters

A loyal customer is precious, but a loyal customer who gushes about your business to their friends, family, and social media contacts is even more priceless. A clever strategy to increase public awareness is to convert your best supporters into ambassadors. Best of all, while it does need major outreach and engagement efforts, this technique doesn't necessitate a huge financial investment.

- **apply guerilla techniques**

A well-run guerilla marketing campaign is the best approach to engage potential clients if your creative capacity exceeds your marketing budget. The concept is straightforward; all you have to do is use novel promotional strategies intended to generate buzz. Examples include placing your business card inside each book about your industry in a library or bookshop,Use data analytics to comprehend the demographics and purchasing patterns of your current customers. Your marketing tactics can be guided by data-driven insights, which will improve your ability to target the proper demographic.

Showcase client success stories: case studies, and reviews as examples of social proof to back up your claims.

Limited-Time Offers: To motivate quick action, create a sense of urgency with limited-time promos or special offers.

Consistent Branding: To establish a distinctive and recognizable identity, make sure your branding is consistent across all touchpoints. Remember that your strategy can make all the difference, even in a sea of commodities. Be distinctive, interesting, and valuable.

From farther back than any of us can remember, personal selling, advertising, and sales promotion have been the essential marketing approaches. But these tested and proven methods for reaching customers also have their limitations, particularly in light of two significant changes that have taken place in the business picture over the past decade:

1. The costs of communication climbed radically. Media costs skyrocketed. And the cost of a sales call, as estimated by McGraw-Hill, rose from $49 in 1969 to $137 in 1979.

2. A new set of options evolved, giving marketers a wider array of communications tools.

These developments mean that the marketing manager can make the best use of the newer methods, as well as the older ones, to respond to increasing top management demand for efficient and effective communication. In particular, the evolving options offer opportunities to improve the precision and impact of the marketing program, sometimes at great cost savings over the traditional methods.

There is no need for us to belabor the all too familiar change in communications costs. On the other hand, little note has been made of the newer options. Thus, in the first section of this article, we will focus on them. Then, in the second section, we will provide a four-step approach for developing a marketing program that makes the best use of both the newer and the older communications tools.

Evolving Options

In the past, the marketer's primary communications tools were *media advertising, direct mail advertising, telephone selling, trade shows,* and *face-to-face selling*. These traditional methods differed in impact and cost per message, with media advertising at the low end and personal selling at the high end. Telephone and personal selling offered flexibility in tailoring the message to the target prospect and in having two-way contact but at a substantial cost, particularly for the field sales force. Trade shows added the excitement and impact of product demonstration but were competitive and temporary in nature.

Whereas the opportunities to "mix and match" the five traditional approaches into a coherent, synergistic marketing program were limited, we believe that the increase in the number of available tools gives the marketing manager the ability to develop a more integrated, tailored, and cost-effective communications program than was previously possible.

The newer tools include *national account management, demonstration centers, industrial stores, telemarketing,* and new forms of *catalog selling.* These tools, used together and with the traditional methods, are leading to a new economics of selling. Let us look first at these five evolving options individually and then at the opportunities they offer when combined with the traditional methods.

National Account Management

A few large accounts comprise a disproportionately large percentage of almost any company's sales (industrial as well as consumer goods and services). National account management can often be applied

(a) if these large accounts are geographically or organizationally dispersed,
(b) if the selling company has many interactions with the buying company's operating units, and

(c) if the product and selling processes are complex. National account management thus is an extension, improvement, and outgrowth of personal selling. In essence, this method is the ultimate form of both personal selling and management of the personal selling process.

National account management responds to the needs of the customer for a coordinated communications approach while giving the seller a method of coordinating the costs, activities, and objectives of the sales function for its most important accounts. It is expensive, but the value to customer and seller alike is high if the situation is appropriate and the concept well executed.

Many people and companies use other names for this approach. Banks (as well as some other companies) call it *relationship management* because it draws attention to the primary objective of creating and developing an enduring relationship between the selling and buying companies. Others call it *corporate account management* because the accounts are managed at the corporate level, although the customers buy from several divisions in a multidivisional corporation. Yet others prefer the term *international account management* because the relationships transcend national

boundaries. We prefer to use *national account management* because it appears to be the most popular and descriptive term.

National account management programs share certain characteristics, depending on the sales situation:

- First, the accounts managed are large relative to the rest of the company's accounts, sometimes generating more than $50 million each.

- Second, the national account manager is often responsible for coordinating people who work in other divisions of the selling company or in other functional areas. (This raises a great many issues of conflicting objectives and priorities.)

- Third, the national account manager often has responsibility for a team that includes support and operations people.

- Finally, the manager calls on many people in the buying company in addition to those in the formal buying function (e.g., engineering, manufacturing, finance) and often gets involved in highly conceptual, financially oriented systems sales.

The first issue that confronts companies considering national account management is how many accounts to involve. At this point the marketing managers need to understand the difference between "special handling" for a few select accounts and a real national account management program. Almost any company can develop a way to give special attention to a few accounts. But a full-blown national account management program requires fundamental changes in selling philosophy, sales management, and sales organization. Often the special handling of a few select accounts by top-level sales and marketing managers will lead to a formal program because the managers involved cannot find enough time for both the accounts and their regular duties.

Once the program begins, the selection of national accounts is an important phase. American Can Co., for example, found that careful account selection helped to define the nature of the program and to ease its implementation. Many companies, including IBM, separate their programs into different account categories depending on size, geographical dispersion, and servicing needs.

National accounts need special support, as do the managers responsible for them. All of the standard issues of sales management arise: selection, training, supervision, and compensation. The job requires people with both selling and administrative skills. Training and supervision must be keyed to the need for both depth and breadth in skills. And compensation—both amount and form (salary, commission, or both)—becomes important.

But often the most sensitive matter is how to organize. Some companies organize their national account managers with line authority over a large, dispersed sales and support team. Some go so far as to create separate manufacturing operations for each account, and the account team becomes a profit center. Other companies prefer to view the national account managers as coordinators of salespeople who report to different profit centers or divisions. There are a myriad of choices between these two extremes.

Demonstration Centers

Specially designed showrooms, or demonstration centers, allow customers to observe and usually try out complex industrial equipment. The approach supplements personal selling and works best when the equipment being demonstrated is complex and not portable. Demonstration centers have been used in many industries, including telecommunications, data processing, electronic test gear, and machine tools. A variant of the approach is a traveling demonstration center in which the equipment (or process) for sale is mounted in a trailer truck or bus. Rank Xerox, for example, once used a railroad train to demonstrate its equipment all over Europe.

The demonstration center also supplements trade shows, with three major differences between them:

1. The demonstration center is permanent and thus can more easily be fitted in a company's marketing and sales schedule. Trade shows, on the other hand, are temporary and are not scheduled for the convenience of any single company.

2. The company can determine the location of the demonstration center, unlike trade shows.

3. Demonstration centers are designed to provide a competition-free environment for the selling process. Trade shows, of course, are filled with competitors.

But the primary benefit to the seller comes from demonstration—often to high-level executives who are unavailable for standard sales presentations. Demonstration centers in some situations, furthermore, replace months of regular field selling. The economic trade-off then becomes partially a comparison of the cost of the center versus the cost of traveling salespeople. Demonstrating equipment or processes often has more impact than describing them. The most effective demonstration centers relate directly to the customer's needs and include a custom-designed demonstration.

An outstanding example of the concept involved the use of trailer-mounted, demonstration-sized versions of Union Carbide's UNOX wastewater treatment system by the company's Linde division. In the early 1970s, Linde used these models (costing $100,000 each) to demonstrate that its system could handle the wastewater of an industrial plant or even a particular municipality.

Linde had available to it all of the traditional communications approaches. UNOX sales, however, had been slow and difficult. After carefully considering the time and effort involved in selling, Linde executives decided that the demonstration units would speed sales, generate some sales that otherwise would be lost, and save the substantial expense of traditional approaches. And the demonstration units in fact accomplished all these objectives.

Industrial Stores

This approach also involves a demonstration of equipment or a process with the emphasis generally on cost reduction, not the creation of seller benefits. Stores are permanent, but the same concept is used by companies that present customer seminars and demonstrations in hotels, trade shows, or other temporary facilities. Here too the idea is to bring the customer to the salesperson. Boeing Computer Services, for example, has used hotel room demonstrations effectively in selling structural analysis computer time-sharing services to engineering firms. The store approach works well when:

- The sale is too small to justify sales calls. A substantial percentage (often as high as two-thirds) of industrial salespeople's time is spent traveling and waiting to see customers. If the sale is small, personal selling is not economical. One way around the problem is to ask the prospect to do the traveling. Thus, the customer comes to the salesperson's location, not vice versa.

- The product or process is complex and lends itself to demonstration.

- The company does not sell many products to the same customer. (If, on the other hand, the company has a large, active account with the same customer, the cost of a sales call can be amortized over the sale of many products.)

The store approach has been successful in the small business computer industry, where Digital Equipment has more than 20 stores in operation and development. IBM uses a similar approach but promotes it differently, using office space instead of retail space and encouraging appointments instead of drop-ins. In November 1980, however, IBM announced a commitment to develop stores more along the evolving concept used by Digital and other competitors. Xerox has made stores a major part of its marketing strategy. Industrial stores vary widely according to product lines offered and approach used to attract people to visit. Xerox carries a wide variety of items, including many *not* made by Xerox; other stores offer limited lines produced only by the owners. Some, especially those in prime retail locations, can generate walk-in traffic. Others are in more office-oriented settings. For management, the stores certainly raise retail-oriented questions—location, fixtures, sales staffing—concerning their operations. In addition to display and sales service, stores can also provide physical distribution and service facilities to customers.

Economics has played a large part in the development of the store concept. As selling and travel costs escalate, the use of stores will become even more popular.

Telemarketing

Telephone marketing is an important emerging trend that companies can exploit in five ways—as a less costly substitute for personal selling, a supplement to personal selling, a higher-impact substitute for direct-mail and media advertising, a supplement to direct mail and other media, and a replacement for other slower, less convenient communications techniques.

Cost savings:

Telephone selling has traditionally provided a highly customized means of two-way communication. Greater sophistication in telecommunications equipment and services, new marketing approaches, and broader applications have turned telephone selling into telemarketing. It still does not provide the quality of a personal visit but is much cheaper. While a commercial or industrial salesperson might average perhaps 5 or 6 fast personal sales calls per day, he or she can average perhaps 30 long telephone calls. The costs are much lower because of the lack of travel. Personal sales calls tend to cost upward of $100 each, while normal-length telephone sales calls cost generally under $10 each.

The cost advantage makes telemarketing a good substitute for visits to small accounts. Fieldcrest, for example, has been using telemarketing in conjunction with catalogs to introduce and sell bed and bath fashions to stores in sparsely settled areas.

Supplement to personal visits:

Some selling situations require periodic sales visits. Often the cost of the required call frequency is greater than the sales volume justifies and, in these cases, telephone calls can supplement personal visits. The visits might be made two to four times per year and the telephone calls eight to ten times per year for a total frequency of one per month—but at a cost substantially lower than twelve visits. Personal visits would be used for the opening presentation of, say, a new line of apparel or furniture or the sale of equipment, while telephone calls would be used for fill-in orders or supply sales.

Substitute for direct mail:

Some insurance sales-people who wish to keep in touch with their customers have switched from using direct mail to the telephone, which gives greater impact—at an admittedly higher cost. For the economics to work well, the person called must be either an existing customer or a good prospect, not just a random name from the phone book. Telemarketing has been successful in selling subscription renewals and other continuity sales and could also aid sales of large consumer durables such as automobiles, swimming pools, and appliances. A Cadillac salesperson might, for example, telephone owners of Lincoln Continentals or Mercedes that are a few years old.

As a supplement:

Telemarketing can add to as well as replace direct mail and media advertising. Many companies have effectively used the 800 telephone numbers in direct mail, television, and print media advertising. Such a program has three advantages over mail replies: (1) the prospect can make an immediate commitment to purchase while the idea is fresh and the

desire for action greatest—and, perhaps more important, he or she can get an immediate reply; (2) it is easier for most people to telephone than to fill in a coupon and mail it; and (3) the selling company can become actively involved in supplying product information to aid the customer's decision making, and the customer can also express concerns to be responded to by the telephone salespeople in future media communication or even in later product development.

The combined media/telemarketing approach has been successful for a variety of products, including specialty coffees, smokeless tobacco, books, and records. AT&T uses the approach to sell many of its products and services. An additional advantage is the quick generation of data about media effectiveness. Within a few days a company or its advertising agency can determine the effectiveness of a new advertising campaign. With mail response, the time lag slows the analysis so that a campaign is generally run longer before review.

Customer-company coordination:

Finally, the telephone can be used as a part of a communications program to tie companies to their constituencies. The responsiveness and convenience of the telephone, combined with its two-way message content, make it particularly appropriate for this use. A dissatisfied customer, for example, can get a quick response to a problem.[1]

Confused customers who need product information can get it when they need it most, thus preventing product misuse and abuse. O.M. Scott & Sons Co. uses this approach to good advantage in its lawn and garden care business. Problems with the product or its distribution become clear to the seller and can be rectified quickly without much loss of the expensive time of dealers and salespeople. A manufacturer can use the telephone to gather information from salespeople or dealers to find, for example, whether a new product is selling well or whether competitors met a price increase.

The use of the telephone in marketing can create junk phone calls much like junk mail in direct mail advertising. For both economic and customer relations reasons, we advocate the use of selective telemarketing, showing good judgment and good taste. Otherwise, the attention-getting quality of the telephone in uncontrolled situations can irritate consumers.

The telephone's particular mix of benefits and growing cost-effectiveness versus other media make it an increasingly important part of the communications mix. Ongoing telephone contact with customers or prospects can produce important information through close communication. And once the line is open, there are ever-increasing opportunities to creatively cross sell complementary products and services.

Catalog Selling

An old approach in the consumer goods market, catalog selling is an evolving method in industrial and commercial markets. Companies active in the office-and computer-supply businesses have found catalogs to be an efficient way of generating the relatively small dollar sales typical of their businesses. The Drawing Board, an office supply company in Dallas, apparently relies solely on its catalog for communication with customers. Wright Line, Inc., a $50 million vendor of computer-related supplies and capital equipment for computer rooms, programmers and analysts, and small businesses, has developed an elaborate communications system that includes personal selling, telemarketing, and catalogs. The 140-person sales force makes visits for the larger capital equipment sales and for developing systems sales. The quarterly catalog generates both fill-in sales of capital equipment and supplies for already-sold systems, as well as orders from customers whose size would not justify a personal call. Customers can place orders by mail, through the salespeople, or by telephone. Most orders come in by telephone and mail. The catalog—a new approach at Wright Line—has improved sales volume more than Wright Line executives had expected.

Wright Line's integrated approach developed through a combination of careful analysis and trial-and-error testing. Management has been willing and able to try new approaches, carefully analyze the results, and commit resources to the successful experiments.

Other industries have also used catalogs, particularly in conjunction with telephone order centers or telemarketing centers. Sigma Chemical Co., for example, uses a catalog to sell enzymes for laboratory use, although competitors generally use sales forces. Other catalog applications include electronic components and industrial supplies. The approach is highly cost-effective in transmitting a great deal of information to selected prospects and customers in a usable, inexpensive format.

It is interesting to relate the development of the five evolving options to the more traditional approaches. Personal selling led to national account management. Demonstration centers and industrial stores are variations on the trade show. Telemarketing developed from telephone selling and the early inside order desks of industrial distributors. And industrial stores and catalog selling are based on retail stores and consumer catalogs, such as those used by Sears, Roebuck and Co., that date from the nineteenth century.

Economics and technology are driving the evolution, and the need for more precise communications programs is encouraging it.

Creating A Program

The newer ways of selling, when combined with the traditional communications approaches, enable marketers to make precise choices in developing their communications programs. Four major steps are necessary for developing an effective program:

- Analyze the communications costs.

- Specify the communications needs.

- Formulate a coherent program.

- Monitor the total system.

Analyze Current Costs

The basic device for understanding marketing costs is a marketing-oriented income statement that divides all costs into three primary categories—manufacturing, physical distribution, and communication—and two generally smaller categories—non divisible overhead and profit (see Exhibit 1).

Exhibit 1 A marketing-oriented income statement statement

This income statement differs from the company's income statement. To be useful, it should begin with the price the customer pays. Distributor discounts are allocated to communications cost (the value of the retail and wholesale salespeople, display, advertising, trade show attendance) and physical distribution cost (order processing, inventory carrying, transportation). If the distributor customizes the product in the field (e.g., adds accessories, cuts to shape, or mixes), the cost of doing so should be allocated to the manufacturing task.

The well-designed marketing-oriented income statement helps marketers determine the role of each set of costs (manufacturing, distribution, and communication) in their businesses. Marketers can then ask questions such as:

- Where should I concentrate my cost-cutting activities?

- What do I get and, more important perhaps, what does my customer get from each of the three functions?

- Do the benefits provided by each function justify the costs?

Marketing executives can thus categorize their businesses as communications intensive, distribution intensive, or manufacturing intensive and can then analyze competitors from the same viewpoints. Avon Products, for example, trades off higher physical distribution costs (sending its cosmetics and toiletries in small packages to its several hundred thousand salespeople) against the higher communications costs of its competitors, which place more emphasis on advertising but use more efficient distribution methods (large sales to supermarket and drug chains that depend on the customer to pick up the order and transport it home). The marketing-oriented income statement helps to analyze communications costs at a strategic, but not a tactical, level. We cannot consider the detailed costs without first specifying marketers' communications needs or objectives.

Specify Needs

Marketing executives must state precisely the objectives of the communications program and also understand the costs of achieving each objective. There are many different types of communication between a company and its marketing constituencies. Companies may wish to strive for four major goals in specifying their needs:

1. Persuasive impact. Two-way communication is more effective than one-way communication. Media advertising by itself, for example, tends to be one way—from the seller to the buyer—while methods such as telemarketing allow a two-way dialogue.

2. Customization. Different people, even within the same buying unit, desire different information, and opportunities for customization vary. Two-way communication, of course, enables the seller to tailor a message to the precise needs of a specific customer at a given moment.

3. Speed. Some information is much more time sensitive than others. An order to a commodities broker, for example, is urgent. And because we live in an era that stresses instant gratification, many customers want to obtain the product as soon as possible after making their choice, even if they have labored over that choice for weeks, months, or even years.

4. Convenience. Almost everybody, from a professional purchasing agent to a child buying a stick of bubble gum, wants convenience in making purchases.

Formulate a Program

Marketers can create the most effective communications program only with a complete understanding of the relationships among both the old and the evolving options. Perhaps even more important than the media on their own is their potential for integration into a synergistic system that uses each to its best advantage. Exhibit 2 shows the evolving and traditional options and their varying impact and cost per message.

Exhibit 2 Comparing the evolving and traditional options Combinations are especially powerful because each medium has a different mix of benefits and economics. It is easy to envision a communications system that uses all 10 of the media and combinations listed in Exhibit 2. To illustrate, media advertising gives broad coverage at a low cost. Direct mail can be used for a somewhat focused message to a specific group of people at a very reasonable cost. Catalog selling provides a great deal of information, particularly for a wide product assortment, to a focused audience. Telemarketing increases the cost relative to options below it but adds a two-way personalized message, convenience, speed, and the best timing. The combination of catalogs and telemarketing mixes good economics, much information transmittal, and the advantages of the telephone. Industrial stores and trade shows offer the benefits of personal selling with the cost advantages of a stationary sales force. Of course, customer convenience suffers.

Again, personal selling provides important advantages at a high cost. The addition of a demonstration center increases the cost but provides important benefits in major sales. And, finally, national account management provides the ultimate communications medium at the highest cost.

Different approaches can be used for different customers, products, situations, and communications needs. Companies that market many products to many different types of customers will generally need a wider variety of communications modes than companies having a narrower product and customer mix. It should be no surprise that companies such as Digital Equipment and AT&T, with their many products, many types of customers, and new technologies to sell, have been at the forefront of the new approaches. They had little choice.

Time is an important dimension in the development of a synergistic communications program for three major reasons:

- In the first place, advertisers should design every correspondence program with respect to the occasions of the item's life cycle. The arranged presentation of a variety in an item, for instance, could require a similarly painstakingly arranged change in the correspondence blend — maybe to underline another utilization or

another arrangement of clients. Client information travels through its own life cycle. At certain places in an item's life, creating brand mindfulness among possibilities may be especially significant, while at different times the essential accentuation would be on consoling existing clients.

- Second, it requires a long investment to execute interchange programs. The movement from beginning up to compelling activity of a public record program, for instance, can require four to five years. The equivalent is valid, yet less significantly, of different media displayed in Show 2. It can require a year to create, test, and cautiously execute a decent media publicizing or index deals program. As a general rule, the specialized techniques with more prominent effect and greater expense per message in Show demand more investment to carry out than those lower in the order.
- Third, cautious preparation after some time includes the raison d'être of all promoting exercises — the client. Clients recollect. Consequently, much of the time changing interchange programs is incapable, wasteful, and confounding. Clients used to dealing calls won't quickly embrace a modern store or a selling program. All correspondence programs should mirror a worry for the client's memory.The mix-and-match process of developing a program from a set of communications media alternatives has four integral dimensions: market segments, products, media, and time. A lack of concern for any of these elements weakens the whole program.

Monitor the Total System

In some communications-intensive companies the cost of communication can be upward of one-fourth of total sales. Obviously, such expenditures warrant careful control.

Wherever possible, managers should gather and analyze all the data related to the communications process. Executives who use industrial stores will have to think as retailers do about such things as traffic (flow of people into the store) and accessibility.

For example, they should monitor the number of visitors to an industrial store, the source of their initial communication, the percentage of "qualified" prospects, and the percentage of sales. Catalog marketers and telemarketers, of course, can monitor such factors as the average size of an order by customer type, the types of products purchased, and frequency of order.

Effectiveness and Efficiency

. More prominent coordination and closer control. Advertisers can likewise wipe out squander through more prominent coordination, as in public record the executives, or through the nearer control conceivable in modern stores, selling focuses, and list tasks than in a customary field deals force. In outline, then, cautious expense examination, exact necessities determination, imaginative program definition, and careful observing will prompt more powerful and effective correspondence with more prominent client effect and lower costs. telemarketing, or catalogs).

3. *Greater coordination and closer control.* Marketers can also eliminate waste through greater coordination, as in national account management, or through the closer control possible in industrial stores, telemarketing centers, and catalog operations than in a traditional field sales force. In summary, then, careful cost analysis, precise needs specification, creative program formulation, and meticulous monitoring will lead to more effective and efficient communication with greater customer impact and lower costs.

CHAPTER 4.

Adapting and Refining:

In the domain of business, change isn't only consistent — it's objective. The capacity to adjust and refine techniques, cycles, and approaches is which isolates the flourishing from the stale. This unique ability, frequently alluded to as variation and refinement, is the foundation of long haul achievement. In this investigation, we dive into the workmanship and study of adjusting and refining inside the always developing scene of business.

1. The Requirement for Variation and Refinement
The cutting edge business climate is a moving territory, impacted by mechanical progressions, financial vacillations, and changing customer ways of behaving. To stay significant, organizations should embrace variation and refinement as fundamental practices.

2. The Versatile Mentality
Transformation starts with a mentality — a readiness to recognize change and view it as an open door as opposed to a danger. We dig into the brain science behind a versatile attitude and how pioneers develop it inside their groups.

3. The Refinement Cycle
Refinement is tied in with upgrading existing cycles, items, or systems to improve results. We investigate different ways to deal with refinement, like nonstop improvement procedures and the PDCA (Plan-Do-Check-Act) cycle.

4. Adjusting to Innovative Headways
Innovation catalyzes change. We analyze how organizations should take on new advancements as well as adjust their whole functional construction to tackle the likely advantages.

5. Exploring Financial Variances

Financial vulnerabilities are steady. Associations should figure out how to adjust and refine their monetary procedures to climate slumps and jump all over development chances during rises.

6. Client Driven Transformation
Shopper inclinations develop quickly. By understanding their moving necessities, organizations can tailor their contributions and informing, keeping a profound association with their crowd.

7. Contextual analyses in Variation and Refinement
Certifiable models feature how industry monsters and new businesses the same have effectively adjusted and refined their ways to deal with conquering difficulties and accomplish economical development.

8. Coordinated Authoritative Designs
Progressive designs are giving way to spry, versatile systems. We investigate the standards of spry procedure and its effect on current organizations.

9. Information Driven Independent direction
Information fills in as a compass in the realm of variation. We dive into the meaning of information driven navigation and how it illuminates versatile techniques.

10. Position of authority in Exploring Change
Pioneers assume a significant part in driving variation and refinement. We investigate the attributes and activities that powerful pioneers show during seasons of progress.

11. Conquering Protection from Change
Change frequently meets obstruction. We examine techniques to relieve obstruction and encourage a culture where transformation is embraced at all levels.

12. Gaining from Disappointment

Disappointment is an unavoidable piece of trial and error. We investigate how disappointments can be important opportunities for growth that lead to refined methodologies.

13. Adjusting Dependability and Readiness
A lot of transformation can prompt flimsiness, while too little can smother development. Finding the equilibrium is basic for supportable achievement.

14. Moral Contemplations in Transformation
Transformation ought to line up with moral qualities. We analyze possible entanglements and moral problems that might emerge during the interaction.

15. The Eventual fate of Variation
As ventures become more interconnected and speedy, we hypothesize on the future scene of variation and how organizations can get ready.

16. A Structure for Persistent Development
We close with an exhaustive system that exemplifies the standards of variation and refinement, directing organizations toward supported significance and development.

In the liquid universe of business, transformation and refinement are not simple techniques; they are the pith of endurance and success. This investigation fills in as a guide for organizations trying to explore change, jump all over chances, and arise more grounded in a consistently impacting world.

Continuous Improvement in Marketing

In the dynamic and steadily developing scene of showcasing, the idea of persistent improvement has arisen as a foundation of progress. With business sectors turning out to be progressively serious and buyer inclinations continually moving, advertisers have perceived the need to take on a proactive way to deal with upgrading their techniques. Ceaseless improvement, frequently connected with assembling and functional cycles, has flawlessly progressed into the domain of promoting, offering an organized system for refining efforts, upgrading execution, and driving improved results.

The Embodiment of Constant Improvement
At its center, consistent improvement alludes to the continuous work to recognize, examine, and correct deficiencies in cycles or frameworks to accomplish more significant levels of proficiency, adequacy, and quality. In showcasing, this makes an interpretation of to a guarantee to consistently survey and tweak procedures, strategies, and missions to line up with changing business sector elements and client ways of behaving.

The Nonstop Improvement Cycle
The idea of nonstop improvement follows a repetitive example that includes a few key stages:

Plan: This stage includes setting clear targets, characterizing key execution markers (KPIs), and illustrating procedures. Here, advertisers frame the guide for their missions, considering their interest group, channels, informing, and objectives.

Carry out: With an obvious arrangement set up, advertisers execute their systems. This includes making content, sending off missions, and enacting different showcasing channels.

Measure: In this stage, advertisers assemble information through different examination devices to survey the presentation of their missions. Measurements, for example, commitment rates, transformation rates, navigate rates, and profit from speculation (return for capital invested) give bits of knowledge into what's working and so forth.

Break down: The information gathered in the past stage is dissected to recognize patterns, examples, and areas of progress. This step includes

distinguishing bottlenecks, drop-off focuses, and regions where the mission missed the mark concerning assumptions.

Change: In view of the examination, advertisers pursue informed choices to change their systems. This could include tweaking informing, upgrading promotion situations, changing focusing on boundaries, or in any event, changing the whole methodology.

Carry out Once more: The refined techniques are then carried out, starting another pattern of execution, estimation, examination, and change.

Advantages of Nonstop Improvement in Showcasing
Embracing nonstop improvement in promoting offers a plenty of advantages that add to reasonable development and achievement:
Adaptation to Changing Trends: In the fast-paced world of marketing, trends can shift rapidly. Continuous improvement ensures that marketers can swiftly adapt to these changes, preventing campaigns from becoming obsolete or ineffective.

Enhanced Customer Experience: Regularly assessing and refining campaigns allows marketers to better understand their target audience's preferences and pain points. This knowledge enables them to create more relevant and engaging content, leading to an improved customer experience.

Optimized Resource Allocation: By analyzing the performance of different marketing channels and tactics, marketers can allocate their resources more efficiently. This prevents wastage of time and budget on strategies that aren't delivering results.

Higher ROI: Continuous improvement helps identify and rectify underperforming areas, ultimately leading to better ROI. By refining strategies, marketers can ensure that their efforts translate into tangible business outcomes.

Data-Driven Decision Making: The emphasis on measurement and analysis in continuous improvement encourages marketers to base their decisions on data rather than assumptions. This leads to more informed and effective choices.

Cultivation of Innovation: The iterative nature of continuous improvement fosters a culture of innovation within marketing teams. Team members are encouraged to experiment with new ideas and approaches, knowing that the results will be evaluated and refined.

Competitive Advantage: Marketers who consistently strive for improvement are better positioned to outperform competitors. Their agility and ability to stay ahead of market trends give them a distinct competitive edge.

Executing Persistent Improvement Systems
To actually carry out persistent improvement in promoting, associations can think about the accompanying procedures:

Information Assortment and Examination: Strong information assortment through different investigation apparatuses is the underpinning of ceaseless improvement. Advertisers ought to screen applicable measurements and use information to recognize regions for improvement.

Normal Survey Gatherings: Booked survey gatherings give a stage to groups to examine crusade execution, share bits of knowledge, and by and large talk thoughts for development.

A/B Testing: A/B testing includes looking at two forms of a mission component to figure out which performs better. This approach permits advertisers to come to information driven conclusions about what resounds best with the crowd.

Input Coordination: Requesting criticism from clients, outreach groups, and different partners can give significant bits of knowledge into the adequacy of promoting endeavors and regions that need refinement.

Ability Advancement: Consistent improvement additionally stretches out to the expertise advancement of promoting groups. Normal instructional courses and studios guarantee that colleagues stay refreshed with the most recent apparatuses and methods.

Benchmarking: Contrasting your exhibition with industry benchmarks and best practices can feature regions where improvement is required.

Advancement Drives: Devote time and assets to investigating inventive methodologies. Few out of every odd investigation will succeed, however the bits of knowledge acquired can drive future upgrades.

Difficulties and Contemplations
While the idea of consistent improvement offers huge advantages, it's critical to recognize and address possible difficulties:

Asset Limitations: Persistent improvement requires a venture of time, cash, and HR. Associations need to figure out some kind of harmony between progress endeavors and everyday activities.

Protection from Change: Groups acquainted with conventional techniques could oppose continuous changes. A change in mentality is urgent to embracing the iterative idea of consistent improvement.

Momentary versus Long haul Concentration: Finding some kind of harmony between momentary mission objectives and long haul key goals is fundamental. Constant improvement ought to add to both quick wins and supported development.

Information Precision and Translation: Depending on mistaken or misconstrued information can prompt off track enhancements. Guaranteeing information quality and exhaustive investigation is essential.

In the advanced showcasing scene, where client inclinations, innovation, and rivalry develop quickly, the reception of constant improvement techniques is presently not discretionary however vital. By cultivating a culture of interminable upgrade, promoting groups can guarantee that their endeavors stay lined up with their goals, reverberate with their interest group, and yield reliable profits from venture. Through the orderly pattern of arranging, execution, estimation, investigation, and change, associations can explore the intricacies of promoting with dexterity, development, and an upper hand.

CHAPTER 5.

Choose Your Channels: Selecting Effective Marketing Platforms.

Businesses today have access to a wide range of marketing platforms because of the quick-paced digital environment. The success of any marketing campaign can be greatly impacted by choosing the appropriate channels. This post examines the crucial factors to take into account and the best marketing platform selection techniques.

Understanding Marketing Platforms in Section 1
It's critical to have a thorough understanding of what marketing platforms are and why they are vital before starting the selecting process. Marketing platforms include a variety of offline and online channels that organizations can use to connect with their target market.

Identifying Your Target Audience in Section 2
An in-depth understanding of your target demographic is the first step in effective marketing. To customize your strategy, identify demographic, psychographic, and behavioral characteristics. This data directs your choice of platforms that connect with your audience.

SectionSection 3: Assessing Stage Choices
This segment digs into the assorted scope of showcasing stages accessible: virtual entertainment, web search tools, content promoting, email advertising, powerhouse joint efforts, and that's just the beginning. Investigate the qualities and shortcomings of every stage and how they line up with your mission objectives.

Area 4: Adjusting Stages to Battle Objectives
Different showcasing efforts have fluctuating targets: brand mindfulness, lead age, deals transformation, and so on. Figure out how to adjust the qualities of picked stages to your mission objectives to amplify adequacy.

Area 5: Spending plan Designation and return on initial capital investment

Talk about the basic part of spending plan designation. Investigate the expense viability of various stages and their expected Profit from Venture (return on initial capital investment). This segment features the requirement for a reasonable dispersion of assets across stages.

Segment 6: Investigating Information and Adjusting Methodologies
Present day promoting stages give an abundance of information and investigation. Investigate how to use this information to screen execution, go with informed choices, and adjust methodologies for improved results.
Area 7: Keeping up to date with Patterns
Showcasing stages develop quickly because of innovative progressions and changing buyer ways of behaving. Underline the significance of remaining refreshed with industry drifts and being ready to embrace arising stages.

Area 8: Contextual analyses: True Models
Delineate the ideas talked about through genuine contextual analyses. Grandstand how effective organizations chose and used promoting stages to accomplish their objectives.

Area 9: Difficulties and Alleviations
Recognize normal difficulties in choosing showcasing stages, for example, oversaturation, stage calculation changes, and crowd weakness. Give techniques to alleviate these difficulties.

Area 10: Moral Contemplations
Talk about the moral components of showcasing stage determination, including information protection, straightforwardness, and mindful publicizing. Underline the significance of keeping up with entrust with the crowd.

End:
Picking successful showcasing stages is a powerful interaction that requires a profound comprehension of your crowd, crusade objectives, and accessible assets. Via cautiously assessing choices, lining up with goals,

breaking down information, and adjusting methodologies, organizations can make significant missions that reverberate with their interest group and drive results in the always advancing showcasing scene.

CHAPTER 6. Overcoming Challenges: Common Pitfalls and How to

Avoid Them

Conquering difficulties is a fundamental piece of individual and expert development. Whether you're seeking after a profession, beginning a business, or endeavoring to accomplish individual objectives, challenges are unavoidable. Notwithstanding, many individuals fall into normal entanglements that ruin their advancement. In this article, we'll investigate these traps and give pragmatic techniques to stay away from them, eventually prompting more powerful and fruitful approaches to defeating difficulties.

Entanglement 1: Absence of Clear Objectives
One of the essential reasons people stagger in defeating difficulties is the shortfall of clear objectives. Without a particular objective, it's trying to devise a game plan and track progress. To stay away from this trap, put forth distinct and feasible objectives. Separate them into more modest achievements, making it simpler to quantify your progression.

Trap 2: Anxiety toward Disappointment
Apprehension about disappointment frequently incapacitates people, keeping them from facing essential challenges. Embrace the possibility that disappointments are venturing stones to progress. Develop a development mentality that sees mishaps as any open doors to learn and get to the next level. By rethinking disappointment, you can beat this entanglement and push ahead with flexibility.

Trap 3: Absence of Versatility
Unbending nature notwithstanding difficulties can prompt stagnation. Being versatile and open to change is significant. Try not to stall out in one methodology or arrangement. All things considered, stay adaptable and able to change your methodologies depending on the situation. This flexibility can assist you with exploring unexpected obstructions really.

Entanglement 4: Ignoring Taking care of oneself
Conquering difficulties requires energy and concentration. Disregarding taking care of oneself can prompt burnout and lessened execution. Focus on rest, work out, and solid nourishment to keep up with your physical and mental prosperity. At the point when you're at your best, you're better prepared to handle difficulties head-on.

Entanglement 5: Detachment
Attempting to defeat difficulties in detachment can be segregating and counterproductive. Look for help from guides, peers, or a local area that shares your objectives. Cooperative critical thinking frequently yields creative arrangements that you probably won't have considered all alone.
Pitfall 6: Procrastination
Procrastination can be a significant obstacle to progress. Break tasks into smaller, manageable steps, and commit to completing them. Hold yourself accountable for your actions, and use techniques such as the Pomodoro technique to maintain focus and productivity.

Pitfall 7: Self-critical language
Your ability to overcome obstacles can be significantly impacted by your internal discourse. Self-talk that is negative can decrease motivation and confidence. Exercise self-compassion and refute unfavorable beliefs with logic. Develop an optimistic outlook that will motivate you to endure.

Pitfall 8: Ignoring Advice from Previous Failures
Every difficulty offers a chance for development. Repetition of errors is possible if past difficulties are not examined and lessons are not drawn from them. Consider carefully what worked well and what might have been done differently. Use these insights to guide how you deal with present and upcoming issues.

Lack of patience is the ninth trap.

Overcoming obstacles frequently requires time. Being impatient might cause frustration and a hasty attempt at abandonment. Develop patience and recognize that progress might take time.

CHAPTER 7.

Capturing leads

In the sphere of business and promotion, catching leads is a central cycle that holds the way to erecting solid customer connections and driving income development. Leads address implicit guests who have shown an interest in an item or administration, and effectively changing over these leads into paying guests is an introductory part of an association's substance. This composition investigates different procedures and strategies for really catching leads and supporting them through the deals pipe. Understanding Lead Catch Lead catch includes distinguishing and gathering data from people who have communicated interest in an item, administration, or brand. This data can incorporate dispatch addresses, names, telephone figures, and that is just the morning. The ideal is to accumulate an acceptable amount of information to start customized correspondence with leads and guide them towards settling on a buying choice.   Making Convincing Substance One of the stylish ways of catching leads is by making important and connecting content. This could be as blog entries, digital books, online courses, recordings, or infographics. By offering content that tends to the problem areas or difficulties looked at by your interest group, you can allure them to give their contact data in return for entrance to this substance.   Greeting runners and Structures Greeting runners assume a vital part in lead catch. These married runners are intended to give unequivocal data and move guests to make an ideal move, for illustration, finishing up a lead catch structure. The structure generally demands abecedarian contact craft, permitting associations to circle back to anticipated guests.   Select In Offers and Motivating forces To empower supereminent catch, associations constantly give pick in offers or impulses. These could incorporate limits, free overtures, downloadable means, or entrance to picky substance. By offering commodities of significant worth, associations can allure possibilities to madly partake in their contact data.

Online Entertainment Commitment:

Online entertainment stages give a strong road to lead age. Organizations can draw in with their crowd through posts, surveys, challenges, and direct informing. By encouraging a feeling of local area and tending to client questions, brands can change over their online entertainment supporters into leads.

Email Promoting Efforts:
Whenever leads are caught, email promoting efforts become fundamental for supporting these likely clients. Through all around made email groupings, organizations can offer extra benefit, share important substance, and exhibit their items or administrations. The objective is to keep leads drawn in and slowly guide them towards making a buy.

Personalization and Division:
Personalization is a foundation of viable lead catch and sustaining. By sectioning leads in light of their inclinations, conduct, or segment data, organizations can tailor their correspondence to give pertinent substance and offers. Customized connections are bound to reverberate with leads and draw them nearer to transformation.

Lead Scoring and Capability:
Not all leads are made equivalent. Lead scoring and capability processes assist organizations with focusing on their endeavors by recognizing the leads that are probably going to change over into clients. This includes doling out scores in light of variables, for example, commitment level, socioeconomics, and conduct.

Chatbots and Live Visits:
Coordinating chatbots and live visit highlights on sites can altogether improve lead catch endeavors. These devices give constant help to guests, answer inquiries, and guide them through the dynamic cycle. By gathering contact data during these associations, organizations can catch leads consistently.

Constant Investigation and Advancement:

Lead catch procedures require progressing examination and streamlining. By checking measurements, for example, transformation rates, navigate rates, and commitment levels, organizations can recognize what's working and make essential changes. An information driven approach guarantees that lead catch endeavors stay viable over the long run.

All things considered, getting leads is a strong cycle that incorporates a mix of essential planning, innovative substance creation, and consistent responsibility. By understanding the tendencies and pain points of the vested party, associations can fit their lead and strategies to offer genuine advantage. A conclusive goal is to foster relationships with leads, guiding them through the arrangements channel and changing them into steadfast clients. Through a blend of development, modified correspondence, and persuading substance, viable leads transform into the groundwork of sensible business development.

Most arrangement specialists intend to find drivers, who are individuals with the likelihood to become clients. One notable strategy for finding and directing potential clients is to use a lead get, which is a design that collects information about individuals who might be reasonable leads. Getting to know what lead gets are and the manner by which you can utilize them to additionally foster lead age could help you with meeting your arrangements goals.

In this article, we overview what lead get is, the method for making a lead get plan and how you can gain ground with lead get.

Related positions Very on
Occasional positions
Normal positions
Remote positions
Basically utilizing position
View more positions Very on
What does lead get?

Lead get is a strategy for get-together information about individuals who show interest in an association and could become clients later on. There are two or three techniques for making a lead get, yet one of the most broadly perceived approaches to using them is to make a design that offers clients the opportunity to introduce their own information to an association, similar to their name, address and contact information. Lead gets can appear on association locales, electronic diversion stages, messages and blog sections.

Related: What Is A Prospective customer? (What's more, How To Qualify One)

Why use lead catch on your site?

Lead catch can be significant for any business that sells items or administrations since it gives an extraordinary method for laying out and growing a client base. With lead catch, you can take data from possible clients and use it to reach them in the future to offer insights regarding items you proposition and welcome them to make buys with your organization.

Lead catch is likewise significant on the grounds that catches can go about as extra advertising devices. You can utilize lead catch as a source of inspiration (CTA) that welcomes shoppers to cooperate with your organization's site and potentially make a buy.

Related: What Is a Potential Customer Following? Definition and Advantages

The most effective method to formulate a lead catch technique

Here are a few stages that can assist you with sorting out a technique for lead catches:

1. Distinguish the goal

While the fundamental objective of most lead catches is to gather data about potential prospective customers, it can likewise be useful to distinguish a more unambiguous objective that you need to accomplish while making your lead catch. There are various purposes for data assembled through lead catches, so contemplating the particular reason for your lead catch can illuminate its plan and guarantee you incorporate every one of the subtleties that you really want to make yourself clear.

For instance, you could make a lead catch with the target of procuring a specific number of deals for a particular item or drawing in more rush hour gridlock to an organization site. Both of these targets are explicit and attainable, yet they can likewise add to the general objective of producing potential customers.

Related: What Are Deals Goals? (With Models)
2. Decide a lead age offer
A lead age offer is the fundamental subject introduced in a lead catch that can stand out for clients. Many lead age offers incorporate a particular insight regarding an item that features its advantages, an inquiry that poses to users to consider how they could utilize an item or a challenge to collaborate with a site or other piece of media. You could likewise offer something important guests can get in return for entering their data, similar to an aide containing supportive data or a limited time markdown.

One of the best strategies for composing a lead age offer is to utilize a source of inspiration that urges clients to investigate an organization's site and present their contact subtleties so a delegate can reach them in the future with more data.

Related: Top 12 Ways to create a Prospective customer
3. Plan the lead catch page
A lead catch page is a point of arrival that presents your lead catch to purchasers. One of the most widely recognized ways of utilizing a lead catch page is to plan it to show up on the landing page of an organization's site. This can be compelling by furnishing clients with the choice to draw in with the lead catch when they start cooperating with an organization, which can urge them to present their data before they pursue.

An organization could likewise put a lead catch page in an email pamphlet or on their web-based entertainment stages to set out additional open doors to draw in deals leads. Attempt to plan the page to be easy to use to urge more individuals to present their subtleties. This could incorporate simplifying the info fields and guaranteeing the page stacks rapidly.

Related: What Is a Business Page? (With Content, Headings and Tips)
4. Distribute the structure on the organization's foundation
When you plan your lead catch page, you can distribute it to the stage where you figure it can draw in the most expected leads. Many organizations distribute their lead catches on their sites, however they could likewise convey lead catches in different types of correspondence, similar to messages or virtual entertainment posts. At the point when you make your lead catch public, it can likewise be useful to incorporate a part for client tributes so clients can leave criticism about their encounters that may be helpful to new guests to an organization's site.

Consider utilizing a spring up to catch leads from individuals pursuing your site. A few associations likewise go through pop chatbots that welcome guests to take part in a robotized discussion about their requirements.

5. Screen and change your lead catch
It tends to be particularly critical to screen the exhibition of any lead catch you make to decide how you could possibly further develop it after some time. For instance, you could find that a specific segment appears to collaborate with your lead catch as often as possible while another segment overlooks it. For this situation, you can update the subtleties you present in your lead catch to attempt to draw in clients in any socioeconomics you may miss.

One supportive strategy for streamlining your lead catch structure is A/B testing. Make two renditions of your structure and shift back and forth between them. Then, audit the criticism you get from each structure to figure out which one performs better. Break down what was different between the two structures and recreate the viewpoints that were best in drawing in leads.

Do you really want assistance with your resume?
Tips for fruitful lead catch
The following are a couple of ways to direct a lead catch:

Utilize different types of lead catches
There are one or two kinds of lead catches that a business can use to produce prospective customers. While the most widely recognized may be to make a lead catch page on an organization site, you can likewise configuration lead catches that gather client data over email, from calls or from direct messages via virtual entertainment stages. Involving at least one elective strategy for lead catches can improve your advertising drive by extending the gathering of buyers you can reach.

Consider the fields you use in your structure
While making a lead catch page, pondering the fields you need to remember for the structure that clients use to present their own data can assist with ensuring your lead catch is compact and just proposes significant subtleties. This can smooth out the most common way of finishing up a lead catch structure for clients and can help make exploring lead catch frames a simple and fast cycle. For instance, assuming your lead catch targets purchasers in the overall population, you could focus on fields that emphasize contact data and way of life propensities as opposed to subtleties like work title or industry.

Screen your wellsprings of traffic
Since a lead catch normally works on a specific stage, it may very well be essential to consider how much traffic that source could reasonably draw in. There are numerous ways of monitoring how much traffic a site or page encounters, for example, surveying a page's presentation in web search tool results and recording the quantity of communications posts on an organization's site. When you comprehend where the vast majority of your traffic comes from, you can plan your lead catch to show up on that particular stage to reach whatever number of potential prospective customers as could be expected under the circumstances.

Related: 26 Viable Ways Of expanding Traffic to Your Site
Streamline your structure
Use improvement strategies to build your possibilities drawing in qualified leads. Division is one key methodology that can assist you with giving potential leads designated catches to urge them to remain on your page. Lead division classifies guests into gatherings, similar to individuals who are new to your site and individuals who've previously made a buy. You could likewise section as per their area or their excursion on your site.

You can then computerize tweaked lead catch structures for each gathering to expand the opportunity of changes. Computer based intelligence instruments can empower your site to investigate guest information in a flash and present them with valuable open doors that line up with their requirements. For instance, computerized chatbots that utilization regular language handling (NLP) innovation to message guests might have the option to qualify leads and direct them to different pages on your site in light of their responses.

CHAPTER. 8

Fix problem

The universe of business is a unique scene, set apart by potential open doors and impediments the same. A center skill that recognizes effective organizations from the rest is their capacity to distinguish, address, and defeat difficulties. This complete review dives profound into the specialty of critical thinking in the business domain, breaking down techniques, contextual analyses, and best practices.

Segment 1: The Idea of Business Difficulties
1.1 Distinguishing Normal Business Difficulties:
Organizations face a huge number of difficulties, from market variances and contests to struggles under the surface and functional shortcomings. Understanding these difficulties is the most vital move towards tracking down compelling arrangements.

1.2 The Effect of Difficulties:
Neglected difficulties can prompt monetary misfortunes, harmed standing, and frustrated development. Perceiving the results of annoying issues features the earnestness of proactive critical thinking.

Segment 2: Key Ways to deal with Critical thinking
2.1 Main driver Examination:
Revealing the underlying drivers of difficulties is urgent. This approach includes digging profoundly to distinguish fundamental issues as opposed to simply tending to superficial side effects.

2.2 SWOT Investigation:
Directing a SWOT (Qualities, Shortcomings, Potential open doors, Dangers) examination gives a thorough comprehension of the business' inner and outer scene, supporting issues distinguishing proof and arrangement plan.

2.3 Plan Thinking:
Configuration thinking stresses sympathy and intelligent fixes. By understanding the requirements of clients and partners, organizations can enhance and make significant arrangements.

Area 3: Contextual analysis in Business Critical thinking
3.1 Apple's Development Process:
Apple's capacity to change difficulties into open doors is exemplified by its excursion. From the edge of insolvency to mechanical strength, the organization's development driven critical thinking has been vital to its prosperity.

3.2 Toyota's Kaizen Theory:
Toyota's obligation to nonstop improvement, epitomized by the Kaizen reasoning, has prompted smoothed out processes, diminished squander, and a culture of critical thinking all through the association.

3.3 Airbnb's Administrative Difficulties:
Airbnb's quick extension was joined by administrative obstacles. The organization's versatile critical thinking approach included teaming up with partners and adjusting its model to follow neighborhood guidelines.

Segment 4: Techniques for Powerful Execution
4.1 Cross-Useful Coordinated effort:
Settling complex business challenges frequently requires input from different offices. Empowering cross-practical joint effort cultivates assorted points of view and balanced arrangements.

4.2 Nimble Approach:
The Nimble approach, starting in programming advancement, has found its direction into business critical thinking. Its iterative methodology permits organizations to adjust arrangements as they gain from execution.

4.3 Information Driven Navigation:

Utilizing information investigation gives experiences that drive informed navigation. Organizations can distinguish patterns, expect difficulties, and approve the viability of arrangements.

Area 5: Long haul Critical thinking Attitude
5.1 Position of authority in Critical thinking:
Successful administration establishes the vibe for critical thinking inside an association. Pioneers who energize development, risk-taking, and gaining from disappointments encourage a critical thinking society.

5.2 Gaining from Disappointments:
Disappointments are unavoidable in business, yet they additionally present open doors for development. Embracing disappointments as opportunities for growth and applying examples to future difficulties is significant for long haul achievement.

5.3 Maintainability and Moral Contemplations:
In the advanced business scene, tackling issues should likewise line up with moral and feasible practices. Addressing natural and social difficulties is becoming necessary to long haul feasibility.

End:
Critical thinking is a foundation of outcome in the business world. By grasping the idea of difficulties, embracing vital methodologies, gaining from contextual analyses, and cultivating a critical thinking society, organizations can explore the intricacies of the market, enhance even with misfortune, and at last accomplish supported development.